Standing in the Pizzicato Rain

Georgina Eddison

salmonpoetry

Published in 2009 by
Salmon Poetry
Cliffs of Moher, County Clare, Ireland
Website: www.salmonpoetry.com
Email: info@salmonpoetry.com

ISBN 978-1-907056-15-4

Cover artwork: Darrenw, Dreamstime.com
Cover design & typesetting: Siobhán Hutson

The publisher gratefully acknowledges the financial support of Writers' Week Listowel and Profile Developments, Co. Limerick, in the publication of this book:

Writers' Week
LISTOWEL

Profile Developments (Est. 1984)

For John,

who is painted in all of these poems

Acknowledgements

Acknowledgements are due to the editors of the following, in which some of these poems first appeared:

The SHOp, *The Sunday Tribune*, *Cyphers*, and *Coming to the Well for Water*.

Thanks to Brendan Kennelly, Eiléan Ní Chuilleanaín and Dermot Bolger.

Special thanks to Ann Egan for her support and editorial skills, and to Hayden Murphy who first published my poems in *Broadsheet*.

Special thanks also to Listowel Writers' Week and Profile Developments, Kilfergus, Glin, Co. Limerick, for funding the publication of this collection, which won the 2008 Listowel Writers' Week Poetry Competition.

Contents

Duet

The sky is drum tight
and rain will begin.
Raising her arms like a conductor
my mother plucks clothes
from the five strings
of her washing line,
rushing to shelter.

Standing in the pizzicato rain,
my father takes his violin
and plays the pegs that remain
as notes
on the stave of her clothesline,
gathering close
the music she has left behind.

Imprint

Remember as children
we left the curtains
undrawn, the room submerged
in night.
We traced fish
on the damp window bay,
moonlight like mercury on the glass.
And how we watched later,
our mouths open,
as headlights suddenly
rinsed the room,
caught our shoal in a net
of shadow,
cast them swimming
around the walls.

We sat in the undertow
small as mermaids,
anchored tight in our beds,
singing, singing.

Haruspicy

Fat as a sequined purse
filled with secrets,
the salmon is wrapped
in tin-foil skin.
I watch my mother open it.
Her knife parts the belly,
spills onto newspaper
a tangle of entrails.
I am nine years old
reading my future
among the blood-soaked headlines.
Her deft fingers say;
'This is how it is to be a woman.'

My mother as Eve

The only time I heard
my mother speak Latin
was to confide
she and Dad practiced
'Coitus Interruptus'
(until they became
quite good at it.)
It replaced
'Vatican Roulette'
after too many
shots in the dark.

The day she confessed to the priest
he raged,
Adam's apple jigging up and down
against his roman collar.
'Your *husband's* immortal soul
will burn for all eternity'.
His hot words spilled
on stony ground.

So, she went home
and saying nothing,
took herself, her husband and his immortal soul
to bed for a threesome,
knowing that afterwards
there would be
one hell of a smoke.

Redeeming Myth in Inchicore

When Mam told me
Mrs Sonnix travelled
every Monday morning
down Ring street,
a swan under each arm,

an image of Lir's children
treading green canal water
swam through my mind.

She broke the enchantment
chiming in that each swan
was sailing its ceramic way
to weekly exile
at the local pawn.

Tailor

They hang from hooks
around my father's walls,
flitches of flesh-coloured
paper. Choosing among them
he lays each section
on the flat cloth,
a butcher's diagram
of jointed meat.
Collar, gore, vent, pleat.
Piece by piece
he chalks their contours;
a crime scene outline
daughter shaped.

Gift

for Alec and May

He stands
expansive with whiskey
in the cramped kitchen,
the chemise suspended
from his fingertips
by shoe-string straps.
A shiver of nude crepe-de-chine,
perfect as unblemished flesh.

The children watch wide-eyed.
His wife wipes hands
across an apron
badged with nappy pins.

Snatching it swiftly,
a conjuror's scarf,
she flings the slip on the fire.
Silk shrivels on hot coals.

Over lipstick coloured flames,
smoke rises,
pale as wasted breath.

In and Out

'Young women want
to sleep with men
my age,'
my father announces
through his Guinness loudhailer.
My mother does not look up
from her knitting.
'Why?' she asks,
considering his eighty years.
'Because they know,'
he answers,
'we don't have Aids.'
'Ah!' says my mother,
continuing to knit,
'but you *need* them.'
Her needles still scissoring
in and out.

Transplanted Aunties

Aunties from England
with funny accents,
unpacking suitcases
full of nylon slips,
Avon soaps, roll-ons,
high heels, Mum deodorant,
hair lacquer,
Opal fruits and Spangles.

Wanting batch-loaf,
Denny's rashers, Mikado biscuits,
Lyon's tea, red lemonade.
Telling us with English voices
'Dún an doras'
to prove they hadn't forgotten.

Never suspecting
that door had
long since closed.

Coventry Exile

One day in each year
my Aunt May
locks the bedroom door,
kicks off her shoes,
removes her dress,
slips out of her underwear,
strips away fifty years
of clipped consonants,
unzips stiff vowels,
sips whiskey.

The careful topiary of her tongue
loosens to an earlier rhythm
of long, untidy grasses,
rampant hawthorn hedges,
the pagan excesses
of roadside fuschias.

Lifting up bare arms
she dances in her Irish skin,
the soles of her feet
beating like bodhráns.

Vision quest

Mystics do it,
take peyote
to commune
with the Gods.

Juvaro people believe
to achieve Arutum,
the second soul,
you consume datura.

Shamans take
draughts of mescaline,
to induce a trance,
channel the spirit world.

Kopi priests use
coca to hallucinate
an altered state
at sacred sites.

Therefore I do not doubt
as an article of faith
when, like the holy carpenter,
you worked with wood

bonding joints,
breathing solvent
in the small temple
of your garden shed,
you saw a vision
of Christ's crucifixion
hanging in the air
like vapour.

Betrayal

That time
I distracted you,
allowed the doctor
jab a needle in your arm,
without warning.
The look of alarm
on your two-year old face.
The pain nothing
compared to the harm
of feeling betrayal
sneak through your veins.
I felt a noose of shame
when, like Jesus,
you turned to me for solace,
and let me kiss
your cheek.

Finding Jesus

for Sez

At Christmas
you kidnapped Baby Jesus
away from His manger
leaving a ransom note
lying in His crib.

Soldiers of Christ,
the nuns hunted for Him,
every locker opened and shut,
doors banging loud as rifle shots
down the length of each corridor.

You imagined searchlights, hounds.
The weight of Jesus
in His school-bag shroud
bearing heavily
across your shoulder.

Questioned, you denied Him,
fear digging nails
into your palms.

Frightened, you buried Him
in a flower-pot grave
on the classroom sill.

The term rolled by stone- heavy,
until Easter came.
You swore you heard Him
rising from His terracotta tomb
the stains of your sin
washed clean.

Curtains

All that time
you kept me in the dark,
not a chink, an inkling
of light.
Sheets of anger
shuttered the room.

Both of us lying
in the concealing gloom
total as blackout
in an air-raid shelter,
listening to rain
tap a Morse code
you wouldn't explain.

The day I tore them down,
found myself
poised in the sunlight,
the ringing applause
finally sounding
'All Clear.'

Ending

My mother knits,
the ball of wool at her feet
a world she sets spinning
with each tug.
It grows smaller.
Her needles tick
through the fuse of wool,
testing the tension.
We listen,
knowing someday
it will stop.
Covering our ears,
we wait for silence
to explode.

Retrospective

for Liam Brady

The door ajar
into a box-room turned studio
after the children had grown,
my father's art.

A slab of wood propped as an easel
on the flat table,
tubes of paint squeezed out,
sable brushes bone dry.
A dust of ash
beside the spent, white comma
of a cigarette.

Light fades behind the window sash
onto a painting, still incomplete,
rinse water in a glass jar
clouded with unused sky.

Sea Change

During my visit
he insists
the nursing home
was once a submarine.

Tells me how cleverly
they have altered it
leaving guide rails
trail along the walls.

Pictures cover portholes
down the narrow corridors.
He feels the swell of the sea
makes him unsteady, at times.

A nearby church bell
chimes another unheard hour
through the complex coral
chamber of his ear.

I look back when I leave,
expect to see him wave
as he did all those years…
he is no longer there.

My father,
slowly submerging,
sounds an uncharted ocean
I cannot fathom.

Waiting

Other days my father thinks
the nursing home is a bar,
greets me with a grin,
'You'll have a jar.'
I smile back, say
'I'll join you for a drink.'
We sit, he makes small talk,
tries to catch a barman's eye.
The nurse wags her finger.

He makes his way to the smoking yard,
points to the roofs of garden sheds
beyond the boundary wall,
explains they are empty carriages,
a railway platform
packed with patient weeds-
his new topography.

I say 'It's time to leave.' He answers
'Stay, I've just ordered two pints.'
At ninety years
there are worse things to wait for
when trains are going nowhere.

Lodenmantel *

i.m Anna Freud

After her father's death
she wore his coat.
Too big for her small frame
she hid in the folds of fabric,
arms tunnelled through sleeves,
fingers pushed into pockets
holding the space
where his hand had been.
Sometimes glimpsing his image
in the diminishing
mirror of herself.

At her life's end
the coat shadowed her bed,
between finger and thumb
a loosened thread
she might unravel
winding the cloth
back into a clew of yarn,
no longer afraid of finding
the only way out.

* Traditional Austrian overcoat.

My Father plays 'Mise Éire'

...but what I recall
is silence as music ends,
your fingers resting, still
margined along the violin's throat.
Now I read
your mantic Ogham.

Smir guailí	*Fires of coal*
Luth bech	*Activity of bees*
Moridrun	*Increasing of secrets*
Cainiu fedaib	*Fairest of trees*
Millsiu feraib	*Sweeter than grasses*
Tosach fregra	*Beginning of an answer*

NOTE:
Ogham is an early Irish linear script used to mark monument stones and associated with incantation and divination. Above is a list of Phrase Oghams.

Stain

The Great War

Despite the photo
being black and white,
the hand
of the girl who delivers
white feathers
to shame
young men into uniform,
is stained deep- red.

Between The Lines

The Great War. 17th April 1917

Difficult to decipher
if it was an attempt
to dupe the censor
when granddad Will
wrote from the French trenches
asking his wife
for a 'little parcel'
of acid drops and bulls-eyes,
emphasis on;
'I just wish for a few sweets,
I want them from you.'

A lover's code.
Language smuggled,
contraband
between wife and husband.

Other words
hidden wounds
he did not send.

Canaries

The Great War

What did we know
of war time deceptions,
promoted from chocolate making
to munitions?
Factory girls.

We pack each empty
shell case with T.N.T.
laugh when our fringes
turn ginger,
coiling out beneath our caps
bright as copper fuse-wire,
our faces tinged yellow.

Doctors conspire,
watch us labour,
not telling
half of us will
never bear children.
Half will fall ill.

The officers despise us,
call us 'canaries'
for our sulphur-tinted skin.
No-one mentions poison.
To think that way is treason.

We sing in our factory cages,
High notes escaping
Light as leaking gas.

Coin

Will Brady, 1917

Rifle held tight as an oar
crossing No Man's Land
riverred with rain,
you reached the barbed wire shore
of the underground.

Crouched among the fallen,
you might have wondered
if the coin given
as recruitment symbol
was the King's shilling,
or an obol?

Namesake *

Let there be light,
and shade in shadowed hatchments
that cross warp and weft
of the shroud-taut cloth.
His image refuses this linen.
I cannot paint Him in.

I believe in pigments,
my brush tip a searching finger
moving beyond figures that flicker
low as votive lamps. I limn
the rising incense of their hymns.
I cannot paint Him in.

I believe in perspective,
the credo of geometry,
a trinity of angles that converges
leading the eye to a vanishing point.
Our shared name on every canvas,
I cannot paint Him out.

* Dutch artist Emanuel de Witte (1617-1692). A life long atheist in a religious age, he specialized in painting church interiors.

Listening

The priest told me
he thought the sound in the ceiling
was the light fitting,
electricity fizzing sherbet-sweet
in the attic space.
Or the insistence of static,
an unsaid prayer searching
the impatient air
for a signal.
And the amber stain
on the ceiling rose
a scorch
from the bulb's over-ripe heat.

Until one morning he found
a string of gold wire
suspended from the shade.
He plucked it with his finger,
his tongue surprised
by the taste of wild honey,
all about him
the steady chanting
of bee music.

Tragedy

Far be it from me
to criticize the Bard,
but what if Romeo had waited
until Juliet awakened?
What if they lived together
for fifty years?

Juliet runs to fat,
body slackened by childbirth.
After forty she grows weary,
a moustache and varicose veins,
each earlobe plump
as an Ethiop's cheek,
form so vast she blocks out the sun
in the east.

Romeo goes bald,
loses teeth
and the run of himself,
back larking about with the lads,
beer belly big as a balcony,
spits out nightingale's bones at the dinner table,
wipes his mouth on his sleeve,
cleans both ears with his little finger.

What if they didn't die?
What if they lived happily ever after?
Now that, Mr Shakespeare,
is a tragedy.

The Poet's Bed

I will make myself a bed, a four-poster,
The framework composed of the bones
Of dead poets, (e.g. Patrick Kavanagh's rib).
I will dress it with linen, exact as a sonnet,
Each sheet stretched tight as vellum,
Blue lines inked on it, with a nib
Sharp as a tooth. For my head, a pillow,
Maybe organza, embroidered with
A stanza or two: the coverlet
A patchwork of villanelle,
Edged all around with haiku.
I will lie among the metred drapes,
Free my mind from all that's troubling
And spend my nights heroic coupling.

This Poem is not about Fish

I have heard of fishes
who perfect the art
of swimming close to razor-sharp coral,
weighing the delicious
tickle of risk on their scales.
Who hitch rides on the backs of whales
not minding where they travel.
Who view the mouths of sharks as caves,
swimming past the barrier reef of their teeth.
Who weave the length of themselves
through fishermen's nets,
like ribbon through eyelet lace.
Who mimic the dimpling of rain on the ocean's surface
with mocking lips.
Who kiss the undersides of ships
to feel the propellers' thrum.
Who flicker in the jaws of drowned sailors
like living tongues.
Who swim against the muscle of tides
to flaunt the flex of authority.
Who lap the flavours of the toxic sea
with casual relish.
Who court the attention of electric eels
and savour the sparks.
Who answer the question marks
of fishermen's hooks with smiles.
Who are never tempted to quench the underwater flame
of themselves in the lonely dark.

Sometimes they rise and see
the oxygen-drenched shore
just beyond the reach of water,
their fins itching like feet.

Falling

One time you eavesdropped
too close to the sun,
tuned to the wavelength
of pilots
pulling you
through clouds, thermals.

The plane bucked
and jumped.
The pilots talked dismissively
of 'chop'.

But your stomach wheeled
as the turbulence grew.
Their voices flamed
with panic.

Your knuckles whitened to wax.
She caught your eye to question.
You couldn't answer,
words caught in your throat
like burning feathers.

Doing it Doggy Style for Yeats

I'm fed up
going down,
doing it doggy style
for Yeats.
Squatting like
a Sheila-na-gig
to finger the spine
of Dylan Thomas
is undignified
at my age.
You need good knees,
strong thighs,
for this game.

'Because it doesn't sell'
The man in the book shop explains,
his pointing finger
sliding yet again
to the lowest level.

That's why I'm swapping
poetry for porn
and the Joy of
reaching instead
for the top shelf.

Aftermath

Someone said:
'You are like
a Christmas cake
decorated in your red dress
and lace collar.'

My limbs sugar with fear.
Will I be broken,
shared and eaten,
icing cracked
like the enamel
on a decaying tooth?

In my red dress
I am a wound
on the conscience,
even when healed
I will leave
a raised scar.